#PerfectlyImperfect

Nine Ways to
Silence Your Inner Critic

Jackie Lopez

Dedication

I would like to dedicate this book to my parents, John Lopez and Maria Avaroma. They have guided me and shaped me into the person I am today and for that I am forever grateful.

Thank you for EVERYTHING!

I love you mom and dad.

Table of Contents

Foreword by A.J. Watkins

Imperfections are not going anywhere. Everybody has one, even your favorite celebrity or athlete. You can choose to embrace or hate them. Hating them can make you feel less than, unqualified, or unloved. Embracing them can give you strength, courage, and confidence.

Your imperfections do not define you, but rather are a part of your identity. The imperfections make you unique. This can be hard to understand because many of us want to fit in. People will stare, make jokes, and assume things about you. But these things don't determine who we are.

God looks at our hearts, not our physical appearance. A lot of people believe our physical appearance determines our value. How we carry ourselves is the true measure of who we are. Don't always believe what others say about you. Your actions will shape who you are.

Do not allow other's opinion to deter you from loving yourself. It can be tempting to believe what they say. They can make you feel less than because of your imperfections. This can be discouraging at times and hurt your feelings. But remember that God made you with a purpose in mind.

I don't believe that God makes mistakes. He made you different for a reason. It may not be clear why right now, but know that He has a plan for you. Know that all the confusion and hurt has a place in your journey. The thing that people made fun of you for, is the same thing that's going to separate you from the crowd.

There is nothing wrong with not fitting in. It's typically the people that stand out that make a difference. Embrace the fact that you are not like everyone else. You were not designed to be perfect. But rather created to be a light in a world surrounded by darkness. You are destined to shine bright.

Wear your imperfections proudly. Show the world that you will not surrender your uniqueness to fit in. You may not be perfect, but you were made in His perfect image. Don't hide from being who you are meant to be. Let the world see the real you.

I used to hate smiling, because of a couple of crooked bottom teeth. Always taking pictures with my mouth closed. People would mention how awesome my

smile was. But I didn't believe it. Occasionally someone would make a joke about them online, but that
didn't hurt me.

You see I had my own belief system about my imperfection. I didn't like it. So no matter what others
thought, I had already made up in my mind how I
felt. It took me learning more about myself to realize
this. I don't have to look a certain way for anyone.
God loves me just the way I am.

My teeth can be fixed if I get braces but my self-worth
would not be fixed. See, you have to learn to love
yourself where you are. Understand that your current
status is not final. There is room to grow within those
imperfections.

Introduction

Loving ourselves exactly as we are is not easy, especially when the world we see on social media constantly shows us of the 'perfect lives' that other people live. To be able to love yourself just as you are, imperfections and all, is tough because some of us have been instilled subconsciously with limiting beliefs about what we can and cannot do. Contrary to all of that, this book was designed and written with you in mind. In the preceding chapters you will find ways and some guidance on how to truly love yourself, even the parts you are not happy with. My hope for you is that you find your inner peace and grow to love yourself just as you are.

The Importance of Self-Awareness, and How to Become More Self-Aware

"We are each gifted in a unique and important way. It is our privilege and our adventure to discover our own special light."

~ Mary Dunbar

Boosting your self-awareness also strengthens your self-confidence. You are able to gain clarity about who you are and what you believe in, and this can ultimately help you live your life to the fullest. Here's a few ways that can help you become more self-aware.

Learn to look at yourself objectively.

This is easier said than done obviously. The point of this is to observe your behaviors and decisions from an objective point of view. It helps to ask a friend that you trust and knows you well. They can help you by providing constructive criticism from their point of view.

Write your own manifesto.

I love this option as it involves bringing in visualization into the picture allowing you to see yourself and your future more clearly. The main purpose of self-awareness is self-improvement, to get better and wiser with each decision and action that we take. You can use your manifesto by reading it before you start your day so it helps refocus your mind on your priorities and values. Your personal manifesto should include the things that are meaningful to you, that you wish to improve upon or carry out as a principle. It is up to you what you wish to do with your manifesto. I have mine hanging up on my wall in front of my bed. It's the first thing I see in the morning; here are a few suggestions as to how it can benefit you:

- As a frame for your life.

- As a mechanism for focusing your mind and reminding you of your priorities.

- As a source of motivation.

- As a behavior modification system, so that you always act in accordance with your values, even during times of stress.

- As a mechanism to keep you striving to achieve high ideals.

- As inspiration to live your purpose.

- As a foundation upon which to build your life.

- As a way to begin to bring a new life—or a new way of living—into existence.

*To see some examples of a Manifesto you can check out my blog at http://jackielovelopez.com/news

Create a daily habit of self-reflection by keeping a journal.

The purpose is to become more mindful and self-aware of our choices and emotions. Self-reflection can be performed in several ways. I personally incorporate it into what I write in my gratitude journal. But for others self-reflecting helps by praying, meditating or even going for a long walk or jog. For me, I find keeping a journal to be very effective. I simply write down how I'm feeling or what I'm thinking, list my roles and the emotions that each role brings, and lastly I write about how my day went (good or bad), it really helps me appreciate the little things in life.

Take your own self-awareness inventory.

In order to become more self-aware and take inventory, you need to get to know yourself a little bit better. These six tips will get you started on building your selfawareness and really learning more about yourself and what you want out of life.

- Figure out what your strong points are. ◎◎
- Take an inventory of your habits (good and bad).

- Make a list of the things you like and dislike.

- Know what motivates you.

- Write down your core values.

- Decide what is relevant to your life right now.

Appreciating Your Uniqueness

"Respect your uniqueness and drop comparison. Relax into your being."

~Osho

How to identify your strengths?

Your strengths can be described as your personal characteristics, that certain trait or traits that allow you to perform at your absolute personal best.

Choose your sources.

Here's how you would begin to identify your strengths if you don't already know what they are, try asking someone you are close to that knows you well enough. Ask yourself or your friend, what it is that you do differently? Identifying your strengths will allow you to improve on it and get better.

Notice your patterns.

After receiving the feedback from your friend begin to look for common patterns as it relates to your strengths. How can you improve or get better? Do you know when you're in your flow? Do you notice your signs of excitement? Mihaly Csikzentmihalyi popularized the concept of "Flow" describing it as the process by which you lose tracking of the time being productive on something that's close to your heart. Journaling would also help to identify your patterns as it relates to your strengths and will help you to stay in your flow.

Create a positive self-image.

This is so important! As redundant as this step may seem, it will help keep you focused when and if you start to have selfdoubt; which by the way, is completely normal to experience. Now that you have identified your strengths and notice what your patterns are you can now move forward with creating a positive selfportrait or self-image of yourself. Write down a brief profile of who you are, what you stand for (your values) and a list of your strengths. Having it written down will allow you to have a clear picture of who you are and have clarity over your strengths and what you should do with them.

Finally, practice your strengths and put them into action!

Create an action plan for when and how you will use your strengths and ask yourself the following?

- How do I use this strength already?

- Do I use this strength in more than one area of my life?

- Could I use it more in another area of my life?

- How can I use this strength in other ways?

Being able to practice your strength in another area of your life will improve your strength and you will find yourself in flow more easily and more often.

Letting Go of Comparisons

"The only person you should try to be better than is the person you were yesterday."

How do you view yourself?

- It's critical to pay attention to how we view ourselves. If necessary we should spend some time alone in order to work on our own self-worth and self-image. So often we get into relationships that end up not working out because we haven't taken enough time to work on ourselves. Having a clear idea of how you see yourself shifts the focus away from others and allows us to really take a look at ourselves in a deeper perspective.

- Focus on you. The best thing you can do is write down your values. What values are important to you? This is what makes YOU special and sets you apart from others. Once, you have clearly identified what your core values are it will allow you to approach things in a more optimistic way.

Don't forget, you are in control. If you are unhappy or not satisfied with the person you've become or realize that you're not able to identify your values, it's okay. You are still in control and you are able to change that.

Why should you limit your time on social media?

- The reason would seem obvious but it's true. Studies have shown that social media draws the attention onto others rather than focusing on ourselves. One of the main internal challenges people face with social media is feeling overwhelmed by others success and accomplishments. This can have anyone feeling discouraged or inadequate but that's why the first part of this section is important. If you have a healthy selfimage of yourself and have a clear vision of where you see yourself in life than others accomplishments shouldn't affect you on the contrary it should inspire you. Regardless, limiting your time on social media will lead you to spending more time focusing on yourself and what you can achieve.

You have probably already figured this out by now but the truth is that social media presents us with a distorted version of reality. Meaning that what you see is probably not real, maybe it is who knows. Either way, getting caught up with what you may come across really isn't worth getting worked up over.

"Comparison is the thief of joy."

Lastly, social media can cause your happiness to become too dependent on others because it can trap you in the mindset of seeking validation from other people. Your happiness should primarily depend upon whether or not you enjoy something and not what others think or how many likes/shares/comments a post may get.

Why should you have a gratitude journal?

- It will change the way you think. When I started my first gratitude journal, I'll be honest, I wasn't sure of what to write about. It started off very short. As I stayed committed to the daily routine of jotting down things that I am grateful for every day, my perspective on everything started to change. And I started to really look forward to waking up, starting my day, and looking out for those little things throughout the day that I appreciate and am grateful for.

- Your body can feel it. I believe this to be true. Even though at the beginning it may seem like 'okay why am I doing this?' I promise you the more open you are to really taking in this exercise, the more you will really start to benefit from the power of gratitude and the magnificent abundance it can bring into your life. As you stay committed and persistent to the task of keeping a gratitude journal and writing down what you're grateful for, your body will start believing what it is that you are thinking and writing down.

- It can help you let go of limiting beliefs and help build strength for when things don't go so well. We tend to see what it is that we expect in our lives and as a result of this, what it is that expect is limited by the beliefs we have about ourselves and about what is possible and likely to happen. If for instance, we are practicing gratitude and incorporating it in our daily lives, our beliefs can change. We have the power to change them by affirming what it is that we are grateful. If things aren't so great, keeping a gratitude journal will really help get you through the tough times. As you begin to practice gratitude, things will begin to turn around. The power of gratitude can help strengthen you through life's challenges and really help get you through them by focusing on the positive things and the things that you are grateful, sending forth positive vibrations and good energy.

Why should you practice selfcompassion?

According to Kristin Neff, PhD, selfcompassion involves practicing selfkindness, engaging in mindfulness, and acknowledging common humanity. Selfcompassion is a practice that has many health benefits, including decreased stress, decreased anxiety, decreased depression and increased resilience. Often, it's difficult to even realize how deeply ingrained our negative self-talk is and how critical we are on ourselves.

- As already mentioned, gratitude falls into this category as it helps boost your mood and minimize unhealthy habits such as complaining, gossiping, or thinking negatively.

- Another way to get your mind off of daily hassles and negative self-talk is to engage in positive, fun activities. It's so easy to get caught up in the challenges that life throws at you but it's important to make time for activities that bring pleasure and relaxation.

- Finally, Journaling is another great way to practice self-care. As you practice writing down your thoughts and feelings on good thoughts or even bad thoughts, it will help bring awareness to how you think about certain things. This process of journaling can help reduce stress and improve your health.

Be True to Yourself

"Wholehearted living is about engaging with our lives from a place of worthiness. It means cultivating the courage, compassion and connection to wake up in the morning and think, 'No matter what gets done and how much is left undone, I am enough.' It's going to bed at night thinking, 'Yes, I am imperfect and vulnerable and sometimes afraid, but that doesn't change the truth that I am also brave and worthy of love and belonging."

~Brene Brown

I love this quote from Brene Brown as I feel it really resonates with worthiness rather than focusing on perfection. This is important because what happens when we start aiming for perfection is that we struggle to find our worthiness and what were really doing is hustling for it. Once you're in perfection mode, you start to trade your authenticity for approval and stop believing in your worthiness.

Brene defines perfectionism as a "selfdestructive and addictive belief system that fuels this primary thought: "If I look perfect, live perfectly, and do everything perfectly, I can avoid or minimize the painful feelings of shame, judgment, and blame."

What perfectionism really is…

I always thought that perfection was just about having high standards for yourself. I thought it was about doing your best. It's not that at all. Perfectionism is really the attempt to avoid all rejection, criticism, and failure. Think about it….

Perfection is about you controlling the outcome of any given situation in order to receive love and acceptance from others. It's really all about fear, the fear of not being good enough.

You see it everywhere, especially on social media. People portraying that they live perfect lives and have it all together all the time. I won't claim that I haven't been there. I remember being in high school and being only concerned about being perfect at everything. I would try to be the perfect student, the perfect daughter, the perfect employee. Oh and most importantly, according to social media, I always had it all together. Little did I know that in doing this I was denying the expression of myself, who I truly was, imperfections and all.

What I realize now...

Life is a practice and in that we are human and we make mistakes. Sometimes we get it right and sometimes we don't. And that is okay.

Give in and surrender.

When we surrender to the mess ups and imperfections, we allow for the seeds of excellence to grow.

"Excellence is that drive toward raising ourselves up to our own highest good thereby allowing our unique gifts, talents, and personalities to benefit the highest good of all."

Unlike perfectionism, striving for excellence is about coming from a place of love. It's about pushing ourselves to act, think, relate, and create from the highest part of ourselves, that is, from a healthy standpoint.

So how do we avoid getting caught up in the idea of being "perfect"?

We can overcome perfectionism by acknowledging our vulnerabilities to the universal experiences of shame, judgment, and blame; develop shame resilience; and practice self-compassion. "When we become more loving and compassionate with ourselves and we begin to practice shame resilience, we can embrace our imperfections. It is in the process of embracing our imperfections that we find our truest gifts and strengthen our most meaningful connections." B. Brown (2009).

Love the Skin You're In and Be Body Positive

"And I said to my body, softly. 'I want to be your friend.' It took a long breath and replied, 'I have been waiting my whole life for this.'"

In my early twenties, I took on a role that required me to have tough skin, which at the time, I'll admit I didn't have, nor did I have any sense of identity. I allowed myself to be influenced by the opinions that others had about me and my weight, especially my superiors. I never realized how much it affected me until later on when I still had trouble seeing myself, my body, in a positive light. It was like no matter what I wore I could still seem to find the imperfection or 'trouble spot.' I see this is so common today when girls take a photo of themselves, the first thing they point out is what looks wrong, rather than seeing the imperfection as beautiful and unique. I believe the media has also placed some influence on this perspective that we have on beauty and perfection, what you must look like in order to be liked and popular. It's like what seems to matter for some is how good we look is directly correlated to the amount of likes you get and that in turn is related to your self-esteem and how good you feel about yourself. Body shaming is much deeper than how you look it is about how you feel about yourself.

It's a self-esteem issue but it is something you can work on. For me it was a self-loving process, it still is. It's a beautiful self-loving process that will allow you to love yourself at any size, even when you gain a few pounds. It's being able to indulge in a good meal and not feel guilty about it. It's being able to take a photo of yourself with no makeup and see the beauty in it. It's being able to embrace your own uniqueness through loving the skin that you're in. Here are a few ways that you can begin to incorporate a healthy self-loving journey with your own body.

Love your body and focus on what helps you feel good.

This could be different for everyone. According to Vivien Ainley, a doctoral candidate in neuroscience at royal Holloway, University of London concluded that people who are able to hear their hearts are less likely to view themselves as objects. In other words, if you're able to listen to yourself and stand inside your body and feel your body, then you can have a good sense of what's happening inside and be aware of what kind of self-talk is taking place. This involves practicing awareness and being mindful of your own self-talk, when you're being critical with yourself or your body.

Be proud of your strong body and appreciate all the things your body can do.

You can begin telling yourself what you like about yourself. You could write this down or just think it through in your head. So often we focus on what's not working well with our bodies, what's aching/hurting etc. If you start to focus on what makes you feel good and be thankful for it, it will switch your state of mind and you'll begin to feel grateful for the body that you currently have.

Step off the scale.

For a long time, I thought the number on the scale mattered. It really doesn't. The number on the scale won't tell you how loved you are and point out your great qualities. It won't remind you that you have the power to choose your own happiness and it most certainly won't help you determine your own self-worth. It is literally psychologically unhealthy for you to allow a number to determine your value and self-image. The scale results could instantly take you from feeling super confident in yourself to feeling super bad about yourself. Its garbage, it's not real and it's not your truth. For one, your scale weight fluctuates. If you are losing weight for a goal you are trying to reach, it's best to go by noticing how your clothes fit you. The number on the scale blinds you from size acceptance that is accepting yourself at the size that you already are. Before beginning your weight loss journey you should still love your body and appreciate it for all it does for you.

Dare to not compare your body and dare to accept your body type.

The other day I came across an article that disturbed me. The title was "How a perfect body looks as seen by men and women." I didn't get it nor was I curious to see what 'the perfect body was.' How could this be? We all have different body types and we all certainly have our own opinion. Comparing our bodies is an unrealistic expectation. I encourage you to start taking steps toward appreciating your body type and shutting off social media from telling you what the right body is or should be. For one, get new role models, follow and search for people who are encouraging women to embrace their bodies. Here's one that I like. It's very short and simple but speaks volume to young women:

> *"I have a belly. And I have cellulite,*
> *and I still deserve love."*
> ~Amy Schumer

Also, put down the fashion magazines and turn off the television, start talking about what you believe is beautiful and begin encouraging others to feel the same way. Little girls grow up insecure because they don't look like what they are seeing on social media and believe that they are supposed to look like what it is that they see and that's what men want. Don't believe that plastic surgery is needed. It's not. Your body is beautiful just the way it is. If there is something you are not happy with then work on it. Get better. Set an example. Be the example.

Use Your Flaws to Guide Your Self-Improvement

"God grant me the serenity to accept the things I cannot change; courage to change the things I can; and wisdom to know the difference."

~Reinhold Niebuhr

Are you willing to change the things you can change to improve yourself?

If you're willing to look past the imperfections and decide to work on improving yourself, you can simply start by taking small baby steps.

An example of a 'baby step' would be something like picking up a book to challenge your mind or maybe just simply being nicer to people.

"The key to success is stringing together enough of the right decisions"

Another step of the changing process is removing the self-limiting beliefs you have about yourself. You can't choose to move forward if you're still stuck feeling self-pity for yourself. Develop optimism and think positive. The possibilities of what can happen when you start making a step towards becoming a better version of yourself will start to appear.

Keep in mind that change doesn't happen overnight. It is a process, a process that you should enjoy. Get around people who are also on this journey and can help keep you accountable. You can learn a lot from putting yourself in the right environment. You can meet people who can introduce you to different resources, places, and books that can help you on your journey of becoming a better version of yourself.

How to accept and love
the things you can't change...

Before jumping into this topic I'd like to address the concept of belonging. Understanding this will change the way you view your flaws. Belonging is the opposite of fitting in. Many of us, including myself, have found ourselves at least once in our lives, suffering between who it is that we are and who it is that we portray to the world in order to gain acceptance.

For instance, when I was in my early twenties I was still discovering myself and not really sure of who I was. I was told there was something wrong with my smile and that I show my gums too much by someone that had a lot of influence over me. At the time, I didn't think much of the comment, I just made the adjustment to "look attractive" when I smiled just so I would be accepted by this person, or at least that's how I thought about it. Until very recently, I viewed the way I naturally smile (showing my gums) as a flaw, an imperfection. If it was caught on camera, I would delete it. My perspective on this has changed not so much of the flaw itself but how the flaw was created in my mind (by someone else).

Don't allow what anyone else may say or think about you or how you look to influence the way you see yourself especially so much to the point where it becomes an imperfection in your eyes. I highly recommend reading the ***Four Agreements, A Practical Guide to Personal Freedom* by Don Miguel Ruiz**; it will completely change the way you feel about your self-limiting beliefs. With that being said, fill your head with other thoughts, positive thoughts! This may require you to take a mental break from social media, meditate, or simply go for a walk.

Find a healthy outlet that will allow you to escape. For me, it's working out or dancing. Many times while even doing the things that we enjoy we can catch ourselves in perfection mode, worrying about how you look or how people will look at you. Take this healthy outlet for what it is, an experience for you to enjoy. Just enjoy the present moment in it.

Find your happy place. This can be a room or simply a state of mind. For me, it is sitting outside in my balcony with a good book. It should be a place that brings you peace.

Love your flaw before you improve it.

The first step of the transformation process is to be honest with yourself. You'd be surprised how many of us could relate to one another when it comes to how we see our flaws. The best thing we could do for ourselves and each other is to look within, be honest, and acknowledge the flaw, whatever it may be.

Admit and express the underlying emotions. Once you identify and express the emotions that are causing you to feel how you feel about your flaw you will be able to change the way you feel about it. Emotions are very powerful especially the feeling of shame which no one wants to talk about but everyone experiences. Once we have admitted and expressed how we feel about our perceived flaw we can begin to unlock ourselves from the suffering or the shame we feel.

Learn to forgive yourself. Many of us have been taught from an early age to be hard on ourselves and that forgiveness is something that usually comes from someone else. However, true forgiveness is when we learn to forgive ourselves and become selfcompassionate this is what sets us free from suffering. When we are able to forgive ourselves authentically, we are able to heal and create real change.

Appreciate and love your flaws. To appreciate something means to recognize its value. When we move ourselves out of feeling like a victim because of our flaws and start learning about ourselves and how to deal with them we can start to feel grateful. And the truth is you can't feel grateful and self-pity at the same time.

Reframing How You View Self- Improvement

1. What does Reframing Mean?

According to *A Daring Adventure*, reframing is the act of taking a situation that you feel negative about and changing how you view and feel about it. Reframing may not be able to change any given situation but at least it provides a different perspective. Once you've changed your outlook on a situation you'll feel more at ease and positive even if the situation itself is negative.

2. What is Self-Improvement and how can it impact your life?

Self-improvement, also known as personal development, is a process that involves personal growth and the enhancement of a person.

Self-improvement or personal development can include a person reaching their full potential or even help a person who suffers from depression, low self-esteem, anxiety or even relationship issues develop the necessary life skills to overcome their emotionally suffering.

Focusing your time and energy into improving yourself can bring forth many blessings and opportunities into your life. It can boost your self-esteem to new levels and ultimately, help you become a better person.

3.   Changing your Self-Talk

What to Say When You Talk To Yourself by **Shad Helmstetter** is a book I highly recommend. It's one of my favorites. It completely brought awareness to the unhealthy, self-destructive conversations I would have with myself daily.

Intentional positive self-talk is the most effective way to replace the negative selftalk that takes place in your mind that makes you feel bad.

Incorporating positive self-talk with short positive statements can reprogram our way of thinking and change the way we talk to ourselves.

Jackie Lopez

4. Monitor your Thoughts

The first step to changing your negative self-talk is to notice the pattern or internal comments of your self-talk.

Let me give you an example of an internal comment that I would make in the mornings:

"I have so many things to do today. Look at the time! There is no way I am going to get any of this done."

Reframed internal comment: "It's too early to tell yet. If anything, I can always prioritize certain tasks and work on what's important and finish the rest later or tomorrow."

Most of the time, the result ends up being that I was able to get everything done that I needed to and even if it meant leaving it for later or the next day it wasn't something to beat myself up about.

When you think about it, it's really not worth the worry to stress about something that hasn't happened yet. Monitoring your thoughts is such a good way of noticing the small comments or internal conversations and then pausing and reframing it to then reflect what you wish the outcome to be.

Failures are Learning Experiences

"The one who falls and gets up is so much stronger than the one who never fell."

At some point in our lives we have to face ours fears, even if we aren't 100% sure of how things will turn out. If you really think about it, a lot of people never really reach their dreams. It's not because of their lack of skill or talent but because they were too afraid to face their fears and at least try.

Treasure your time.

- Sometimes valuing your time means you have to say no to certain things or else you won't be able to prioritize the things that are important to you.

- Don't get distracted so easily. Distractions can cause major interruptions throughout our day which keep us away from being productive.

- It's okay to schedule yourself some quiet time. There is no reason for us to always be reachable all the time. The best thing for us to do is to be present in the moment, focusing our attention to the tasks and people that are in front of us. If we are readily available for every call and email, people will expect it to be this way every single time.

- Stick to your scheduled time limits. Doing this keeps you on track and keeps you productive.

- Keep your word and be on time. Arriving late not only gives off a bad impression but it also shows people you don't value your time or theirs. Hold yourself and others accountable to being on-time. When others are late, reschedule at a time that is convenient for you. It will show others that your time is valuable and not to be wasted.

Push yourself harder.

- If you think about it, every winner was once a beginner. So to put it in perspective, mistakes aren't really as bad as they seem. Mistakes can be viewed as a form of practice. As someone who once considered herself a perfectionist, I used to hold back from putting myself out there because I didn't want to make mistakes. The truth is that the faster you get comfortably acquainted with practicing and making mistakes, the faster you will learn the necessary skills needed to become a master in whatever it is that you are pursuing.

- Positive thinking creates positive results. In order to accomplish anything we must first believe in ourselves. Even though we may not always have control over every circumstance we do have the power to change the way we think about something that we may not like. Things will always work out best for those who make the best out of their situations, positive and negative.

"Success is moving from one failure to another with no loss of enthusiasm."
-Winston Churchill

Success is always closer than it seems. Don't allow failures and mistakes to stop you, it should serve as your motivation to keep pushing forward. This is what it means to be resilient. According to the Merriam-Webster dictionary, to be resilient means "being able to become, strong, healthy, or successful again after something bad has happened". You can learn from each mistake that you make and every time you make one, take it as you are one step closer to your goal. The only downfall about the failing process is if you choose to quit and not go after your goals because you believe that it's too difficult or are simply scared of messing it up again. "Failure is not falling down; failure is staying down when you have the choice to get back up." (marcandangel.com)

Owning up to your failures.

- The first step to owning up to your failure is to accept that making mistakes is a part of life, it happens to everyone. Know that you are not your failures and you shouldn't feel like it defines who you are and what you are capable of.

- A self-assessment can help tremendously in helping you move from point A to point B, knowing where you lack and where you can improve is critical to your success.

- Pick yourself up and keep it moving. Failing or making mistakes is a painful and vulnerable experience but it is the actual experience of learning from our failures that will guide us towards success.

Failure is overrated.

- Life's best lessons are learned unexpectedly. I mean, that's the best way to look at the challenges and obstacles that life throws at us, as life lessons to learn and grow from.

- Not getting what you want can be a blessing. There were many times when I felt so crushed by missing certain opportunities or not getting something that I thought I wanted at the time. It wasn't until much later that I realized it was a blessing that I didn't get what I wanted. You may not be perfect, but God's plan for you is.

- There is no success without failure. Failure is something we all don't welcome very well. Merriam-Webster defines failure as the 'lack of success.' However, I believe we don't give failure the credit it deserves. Failure can play a critical role in our growth as humans and help us towards our path to success, if we allow it to.

I have not failed 10,000 times. I have successfully found 10,000 ways that will not work.

~Thomas Edison

The world will never change/ unless you change.

- You have the capacity to create your own happiness. Don't wait on something or someone to come along to make you happy. True happiness comes from within.

- If you are out of your comfort zone and going for your goals, you are making progress.

- Be resilient, move on and take on another challenge. I remember how horrible I felt after bombing a job interview (something I wanted so bad at the time). I felt down but I knew the best thing for me to do was to tell myself I am resilient and take on another challenge. I didn't immediately but I started to focus on a new challenge which helped me get over the previous obstacle I was facing. I understood that it wasn't that I didn't get it; it was the feeling of not getting it. You know, the messy emotions you start to feel like shame and vulnerable. Once I was aware of what is was; it helped me move on a lot quicker. I then felt ready to take on another challenge. There is something so powerful that takes place when you decide to move past something that once had you down. In my opinion, the most beautiful and courageous thing you can do in life is to rise above the things that everyone would've expected to destroy you; the things you thought would destroy you. Now that is something to be proud of.

Taking Things Less Seriously

"To make mistakes is human; to stumble is commonplace;
to be able to laugh at yourself is maturity."
~William Arthur Ward

Life has a sense of humor.

- Life has its ups and downs and has a funny way of playing with us.

- Taking life too seriously can become really stressful and send you on a downward spiral that doesn't seem to stop.

- Just learn to play along with the obstacles that life throws at you and it will make life seem more delightful.

When I reflect now on how life's challenges affected me and how everything ended up turning out, I've learned to be more light hearted about things and that it wasn't worth getting worked up over.

People matter.

- Even though I have always considered myself to be an introvert, one of my main core values is connection. The reason for this is because when I feel a deep, genuine connection with someone I feel closer to them.

- When you get out of your own head and look around you, you will see that we are all humans striving for connection and ultimately trying our best whether we are a mom/dad, a wife/husband, a student/employee, a daughter/son. We are all doing our best for ourselves and for our families.

- Certainly we are all different but we all have a story. Stories, that when shared authentically, can create connection and we can also learn from other people sharing their vulnerability and experiences with us.

Stress is a killer.

- Taking life too seriously can be so stressful and draining. Incorporating flexibility into your daily routine can lighten things up.

- You can also learn techniques on how to cope with stress. Some techniques that have helped me a lot is meditation and having a To-Do list. Adding meditation into my life has made me more calm and peaceful. To- Do lists have helped me be more productive with my time and it also helps me stay organized.

- Listening to music can also alter your mood especially if you sing along or dance. I feel like listening to your favorite song and dancing along can instantly cheer you up because you are now changing your body's physical state.

Let it go.

- Learn something new instead of beating yourself about something you don't know or haven't mastered. Invest your time into learning a new skill. It will redirect your energy into something positive instead of dwelling on something that makes you feel inadequate.

- Change your point of view. For everything that occurs in your life, positive or negative you have the choice to find the root cause and turn it into a blessing in disguise rather than carrying it on as a burden.

- Focus on something you can control rather than dwelling on something you cannot. Here are some examples: Try meditation which can bring you back to the present. This practice helps me with mindfulness and helps me feel centered. Another option is engaging in something physical which decreases your stress hormones and increases endorphins which can improve your state of mind.

"If you let go a little, you will have a little peace. If you let go a lot, you will have a lot of peace."
~Ajahn Chah

You are Praiseworthy — Praise Yourself for the Things You Do Achieve

"Beauty is when you can appreciate yourself. When you love yourself, that's when you're most beautiful."

~Zoe Kravitz

Take care of yourself (treat yourself).

In my early twenties I believed in living a fast paced life and taking no breaks or time off. I was always on the go, working two jobs and going to school full-time. I was constantly stressed and viewed "making time for myself" as a waste of time. It wasn't until later that I realized how important making time for yourself and taking care of your body actually was. Now, it's a part of my daily life and rarely do I feel stressed or have anxiety, even if I am having a busy day. Some tips for taking care of yourself and cultivating a healthy lifestyle that I found to be life changing for me include:

- Eating healthy, getting enough sleep, exercising regularly and avoid drugs and alcohol. Manage your stress and anxiety.

- Practice good hygiene. "Good hygiene is important for social, medical, and psychological reasons in that it not only reduces the risk of illness, but it also improves the way others view you and how you view yourself."

- Consider joining a support group and see your friends to build your sense of belonging.

- Make sure you treat yourself and do something that you enjoy every day, even if it's something small. Whether that might mean dancing, singing, watching a favorite TV show, working in the garden, painting or reading, etc.

- Find ways to relax, like meditation, yoga, getting a massage, taking a bubble bath, do whatever works for you.

Cultivate your inner advocate.

Your inner advocate is your other voice, the one that defends you and protects you when your inner self critic is trying to judge you and put you down.

We could all use an inner advocate, another voice that's always on our side; that would prevent us from beating ourselves up.

While it may be difficult to permanently get rid of your inner critic, you can surely work on being more kind to yourself by cultivating your inner advocate. Through the work of Kristen Neff, I've learned that these two voices have the same intention to look after us but through different methods. The inner self critic tries to achieve the ends by forcing, shaming, and judging. Your inner advocate uses kindness, encouragement, and love.

Remind yourself of your good qualities (give yourself recognition).

When you accomplish something you are proud of, take a moment to really take it in and enjoy it. Often times, we are quick to acknowledge someone else's accomplishments before our own. Here are a few ways to remind yourself of your great qualities.

- Write yourself a note (positive affirmation) and keep it with you. This can be helpful when you're caught up in a moment and are not feeling your best. Read it, out loud preferably.

- Write compliments on post-it notes and hang them on your mirror, closet, or at your desk (the more places the better).

- Take time to fix yourself and do your makeup in the morning.

- Most importantly, reward yourself by doing something that makes you happy.

Believe in yourself.

They say that the strongest factor for success is self-esteem; believing that you can do it, believing that you deserve it and believing that you will get it.

Identify and ease your doubts. Continue to feed your mind with what you desire and eliminate all thoughts of doubt from your mind. Faith comes by hearing. Fill your ears with words that support what it is that you want to believe about yourself.

Trust and love yourself. Be kind to yourself. You are more worthy than you give yourself credit for.

Give yourself permission to attempt again... and fail forward. Unfortunately, self-doubt doesn't permanently disappear forever, I wish. Though, if you cultivate a healthy habit of positive self-talk, dealing with self! doubt will be easier. It will surely be there when you are outside of your comfort zone and whenever you strive to do something amazing. Your doubts are only thoughts, not your future. Sure, something may go wrong. But if you never try, you're losing an opportunity to improve yourself and your life.

Acknowledgements

I would like to thank my parents and JeanCarlo Perez for being my support system this past year. You guys have been so awesome through this process which I believe could not have been done without you. THANK YOU, I love you guys.

I would like to thank Taurea Avant for creating the Show Your Success Workshops which was the first time I believed I could do this. The system Taurea created is brilliant and helped me out SOOO much. Thank you Taurea, I appreciate all that you do for System Mastery Students.

I'm so grateful to the people that helped me create the book cover and website, Natalie and Denis Pereira. You guys did amazing! Thank you to the photographer of the book cover, Jenna Kneeves and the makeup artist, Natasha Armada for making the book cover come to life. I love and appreciate you ladies.

Lastly, but most importantly, the first people to invest in me and in my dream, my preorders. Thank you to Vanessa Black, Maria Esther Mendez Avaroma, Michelle Hernandez, and Allyse Gibson for your support. I love you guys!

Sources

Letting Go of Comparisons

http://elitedaily.com/life/limit-time-onsocial-media/1036660/

You Are Praiseworthy

http://www.mentalhealthamerica.net/taking-good-care-yourself

http://youqueen.com/life/personaldevelopment/5-ways-to-remind-yourselfhow-great-you-are/

http://tinybuddha.com/blog/how-tobelieve-in-yourself-in-the-face-ofoverwhelming-self-doubt/

https://getkind.net/2016/08/28/10-waysto-be-kinder-to-your-self/

Use Your Flaws to Guide Your Self-Improvement

http://www.adaringadventure.com/whatsreframing/

http://servingjoy.com/take-baby-steps-toimprove-yourself/

http://www.success.com/article/how-to-change-yourself-in-positive-ways

http://www.wikihow.com/Embrace-Your-Flaws

http://liveboldandbloom.com/10/selfconfidence/boost-self-esteem-loving-your-flaws-and-failures

http://thoughtcatalog.com/briannaewiest/2013/05/how-to-accept-what-you-cant-change/

http://www.selfgrowth.com/articles/love_your_flaws

Appreciating Your Uniqueness

http://www.actionforhappiness.org/takeaction/find-your-strengths-and-focus-on-using-them

http://www.huffingtonpost.com/adamgrant/discover-your-strengths_b_3532528.html

https://www.americanexpress.com/us/small-business/openforum/articles/the-simple-secret-to-identifying-your-strengths-rajesh-setty/

Self-Awareness

http://www.theacornstash.com/how-well-do-you-know-yourself-six-tips-for-building-self-awareness

http://lifehacker.com/the-importance-ofself-awareness-and-how-to-become-mor-1624744518

http://www.change-managementcoach.com/self-awareness.html

https://daringtolivefully.com/personalmanifesto

http://www.lifehack.org/articles/productivity/10-more-insanely-awesome-inspirational-manifestos.html

Body Positive

http://whole9life.com/2013/04/repost-break-up-with-your-scale/

http://www.thebodypositive.org/

Failures Are Learning Experiences

https://timemanagementninja.com/2014/06/5-ways-youre-telling-people-your-time-isnt-valuable/

http://www.marcandangel.com/2012/04/05/keep-you-motivated-after-a-mistake/

Taking Things Less Seriously

http://thelilaclounge.com/8-ways-to-let-go-of-perfect/

http://www.lessordinaryliving.com/blog/stop-taking-life-too-seriously-%E2%80%93-5-ways-to-enjoy-thejourney/

http://www.wikihow.com/Stop-Taking-Life-Too-Seriously

http://tinybuddha.com/blog/40-ways-tolet-go-and-feel-less-pain/

Be True To Yourself

http://brenebrown.com/2009/03/18/2009318perfectionism-andclaiming-shame-html/

http://tinybuddha.com/blog/one-thing-need-know-overcome-perfectionism/